Wonders!!! Past, present, and to come! Being the strange prophecies, and uncommon predictions of the famous Mother Shipton, ... Copied from the original scroll delivered by her to the Abbot of Beverly

Mother Shipton

Wonders!!! Past, present, and to come! Being the strange prophecies, and uncommon predictions of the famous Mother Shipton, ... Copied from the original scroll delivered by her to the Abbot of Beverly: ... To which is prefixed an account of her life and o

Shipton, Mother (Ursula)
ESTCID: T090173
Reproduction from British Library
With a half-title.
London : re-printed for S. Baker, and sold by I. Denley; J. Riebau; H. Setchel; J. Aldrich; I. Abel, Northampton; and may be had of all other booksellers in town and country, 1797.
23,[1]p.,plates : ports. ; 12°

Gale ECCO Print Editions

Relive history with *Eighteenth Century Collections Online*, now available in print for the independent historian and collector. This series includes the most significant English-language and foreign-language works printed in Great Britain during the eighteenth century, and is organized in seven different subject areas including literature and language; medicine, science, and technology; and religion and philosophy. The collection also includes thousands of important works from the Americas.

The eighteenth century has been called "The Age of Enlightenment." It was a period of rapid advance in print culture and publishing, in world exploration, and in the rapid growth of science and technology – all of which had a profound impact on the political and cultural landscape. At the end of the century the American Revolution, French Revolution and Industrial Revolution, perhaps three of the most significant events in modern history, set in motion developments that eventually dominated world political, economic, and social life.

In a groundbreaking effort, Gale initiated a revolution of its own: digitization of epic proportions to preserve these invaluable works in the largest online archive of its kind. Contributions from major world libraries constitute over 175,000 original printed works. Scanned images of the actual pages, rather than transcriptions, recreate the works *as they first appeared.*

Now for the first time, these high-quality digital scans of original works are available via print-on-demand, making them readily accessible to libraries, students, independent scholars, and readers of all ages.

For our initial release we have created seven robust collections to form one the world's most comprehensive catalogs of 18th century works.

Initial Gale ECCO Print Editions collections include:

History and Geography
Rich in titles on English life and social history, this collection spans the world as it was known to eighteenth-century historians and explorers. Titles include a wealth of travel accounts and diaries, histories of nations from throughout the world, and maps and charts of a world that was still being discovered. Students of the War of American Independence will find fascinating accounts from the British side of conflict.

Social Science
Delve into what it was like to live during the eighteenth century by reading the first-hand accounts of everyday people, including city dwellers and farmers, businessmen and bankers, artisans and merchants, artists and their patrons, politicians and their constituents. Original texts make the American, French, and Industrial revolutions vividly contemporary.

Medicine, Science and Technology
Medical theory and practice of the 1700s developed rapidly, as is evidenced by the extensive collection, which includes descriptions of diseases, their conditions, and treatments. Books on science and technology, agriculture, military technology, natural philosophy, even cookbooks, are all contained here.

Literature and Language
Western literary study flows out of eighteenth-century works by Alexander Pope, Daniel Defoe, Henry Fielding, Frances Burney, Denis Diderot, Johann Gottfried Herder, Johann Wolfgang von Goethe, and others. Experience the birth of the modern novel, or compare the development of language using dictionaries and grammar discourses.

Religion and Philosophy
The Age of Enlightenment profoundly enriched religious and philosophical understanding and continues to influence present-day thinking. Works collected here include masterpieces by David Hume, Immanuel Kant, and Jean-Jacques Rousseau, as well as religious sermons and moral debates on the issues of the day, such as the slave trade. The Age of Reason saw conflict between Protestantism and Catholicism transformed into one between faith and logic -- a debate that continues in the twenty-first century.

Law and Reference
This collection reveals the history of English common law and Empire law in a vastly changing world of British expansion. Dominating the legal field is the *Commentaries of the Law of England* by Sir William Blackstone, which first appeared in 1765. Reference works such as almanacs and catalogues continue to educate us by revealing the day-to-day workings of society.

Fine Arts
The eighteenth-century fascination with Greek and Roman antiquity followed the systematic excavation of the ruins at Pompeii and Herculaneum in southern Italy; and after 1750 a neoclassical style dominated all artistic fields. The titles here trace developments in mostly English-language works on painting, sculpture, architecture, music, theater, and other disciplines. Instructional works on musical instruments, catalogs of art objects, comic operas, and more are also included.

The BiblioLife Network

This project was made possible in part by the BiblioLife Network (BLN), a project aimed at addressing some of the huge challenges facing book preservationists around the world. The BLN includes libraries, library networks, archives, subject matter experts, online communities and library service providers. We believe every book ever published should be available as a high-quality print reproduction; printed on-demand anywhere in the world. This insures the ongoing accessibility of the content and helps generate sustainable revenue for the libraries and organizations that work to preserve these important materials.

The following book is in the "public domain" and represents an authentic reproduction of the text as printed by the original publisher. While we have attempted to accurately maintain the integrity of the original work, there are sometimes problems with the original work or the micro-film from which the books were digitized. This can result in minor errors in reproduction. Possible imperfections include missing and blurred pages, poor pictures, markings and other reproduction issues beyond our control. Because this work is culturally important, we have made it available as part of our commitment to protecting, preserving, and promoting the world's literature.

GUIDE TO FOLD-OUTS MAPS and OVERSIZED IMAGES

The book you are reading was digitized from microfilm captured over the past thirty to forty years. Years after the creation of the original microfilm, the book was converted to digital files and made available in an online database.

In an online database, page images do not need to conform to the size restrictions found in a printed book. When converting these images back into a printed bound book, the page sizes are standardized in ways that maintain the detail of the original. For large images, such as fold-out maps, the original page image is split into two or more pages

Guidelines used to determine how to split the page image follows:

• Some images are split vertically; large images require vertical and horizontal splits.
• For horizontal splits, the content is split left to right.
• For vertical splits, the content is split from top to bottom.
• For both vertical and horizontal splits, the image is processed from top left to bottom right.

MOTHER SHIPTON's,

LIFE,

AND

CURIOUS PROPHECIES.

S'r, tho' from Heav'n remote, to Heaven could move,
With ftrength of Mind, and tread th' Abyss above,
And penetrate, with her interior light,
Thofe uppei depths which nature hid from Sight;
And what she had obferv'd and learn'd from thence,
Lov'd in familiar language to difpenfe —DRYDEN.

(Price Sixpence.)

MOTHER SHIPTON'S STATUE

𝔚𝔬𝔫𝔡𝔢𝔯𝔰 !!!

PAST, PRESENT, AND TO COME!

BEING THE

Strange Prophecies, and Uncommon Predictions

OF THE

FAMOUS

MOTHER SHIPTON,

Generally known by the Appellation

OF THE

YORKSHIRE PROPHETESS.

Copied from the Original Scroll delivered by her to the Abbot of Beverly. Privately preserved, in a Noble Family for many Years, and lately discovered among other *Curious* and *Valuable* Manuscripts.

TO WHICH IS PREFIXED

An Account of her Life and other Prophecies, with their proper Explanations.

Embellished with her Portrait from an Original Drawing, and a Correct View of her Statue near the City of York.

London:

Re-printed for S. BAKER, and sold by I. DENLEY, No. 10, Gate Street, Lincoln's Inn Fields, J RIEBAU, Strand; H SETCHEL, King Street, Covent Garden, J ALDRICH, Piazza, Covent Garden, I. ABEL, Northampton, and may be had of all other Booksellers in Town and Country.

1797.

THE FAMOUS MOTHER SHIPTON

Publish'd as the act directs by J Denley & S Baker April 1 1797

MOTHER SHIPTON's LIFE,

AND

CURIOUS PROPHECIES.

VARIOUS have been the conjectures of mankind, in this part of the world, concerning our famous prophetefs. Some have reported her father was a Necromancer, and her mother a Witch, so she had the Black Art by Succefsion, others, of a more exalted turn, pretend, that her mother, being left an orphan about the age of Sixteen, took a walk into the fields, and sitting down upon a green Bank, under a shade, to sooth her Melancholy, a Dæmon, in the fhape of a handsome young man, appeared before her, and enquired the cause of her diftrefs, fhe answered him, her parents and friends were dead, and fhe difpaired of a livelihood, upon which, under a pretence of being a person of figure and fortune, he gave her to underftand, if fhe would comply with his defires he would preferve her above the reach of want as long as fhe lived ; fhe readily condescended, received him into her apartment, and entertained him as a Gallant, in return, he bid her sweep the floor once every day after his departure, fhe punctually observed his directions; and never failed finding a quantity of nine-pences, three-pences, and other *odd* kind of pieces fufficient for all her occafions.

At length the embraces of hei Infernal Gallant produced a Pregnancy, and at the time of her delivery, such a terrible ftorm of Thunder and Lightning appeared, that houses were beat down, trees fhattered, and the very features of the child were so warped and distorted, that it appeared the very mafter-piece of deformity.

But these, and many other reports of the like nature, are as romantic as the Fabulous intrigues of the Heathen Gods and Goddeffes. The Genuine account is, fhe w's born in *July* 1488, in the reign of King Henry VII. near *Knaresborough*, in the County of *York*. She was, like the reft of female Infants, her Mother's daughter by a man, and was Baptised by the Abbot of *Beverly*, by the name of *Ursula Sonthiel;* her ftature was larger than common, her body crooked, her face frightful ; but her underftanding extraordinary.

The

The vulgar relations of her life and actions are equally extravagant with those of her Birth before-mentioned, but as those Legends are so ridiculous and trifling, the ingenuous reader will excuse us if we pafs 'em by, and proceed to more probable and authentic information.

'Tis generally held, by moft of the firft quality and beft judgment in the County, that fhe was a person of an ordinary education, but great piety, and that fhe was Supernaturally endowed with an uncommon Penetration into Things, for which fhe became so famous, in time, that great numbeis of all ranks and degrees resorted to her Habitation to hear her Wonderful Discoveries.

We find nothing particularly Remarkable of her till fhe arrived at the age of twenty four years, when fhe was courted by one *Toby Shipton*, a Builder of *Skipton*, a Village fituate four miles north of the City of *York*, who soon after married her, and from this match fhe afterwards derived the name of Mother *Shipton*.

After her Marriage her fame increased more than ever, the events proved the truth of her Predictions, and many began to commit them to Writing.

The firft remarkable Prophecy recorded of

her's, is that upon Cardinal *Wolsey;* the ftory runs as follows.

   She was told, the Cardinal intended to remove his refidence to *York* (that being his Archbifhop-rick) upon wh.ch fhe publickly gave out, *" he fhould never reach the City"* This report coming to the Cardinal's ear, he sent three gen-tlemen, or lords of his retinue to her to enquire the truth of it, and to menace her if fhe persisted in it, these three came disguised to a Village, a mile Weft of the City called *Dring Houses,* and leaving their horses, they took a guide to direct them to her house; upon their knocking at the door, 'tis said fhe called out from within, *come in Mr. Beasly* (that being the name of the guide *(and the three noble Lords with you."* This discovery very much surprized them; but, when they were enter'd, fhe called each by his name, and presented 'em with Cakes and Ale. They signified to her, if fhe knew their errand fhe would hardly treat 'em so handsomely. *" You gave out"* say they, *" the Cardinal fhould never see York"* " no," fhe replies, " *I said he might see it, but never come to it."* They return, *" when he does come he'll certainly burn thee;"* then, taking her linen Handkerchief off her head, *" if this burn"* says fhe, *" so fhall I,"*

an!

and cafting it into the fire before 'em, fhe let it
lie in the flames a quarter of an hour, and taking
it out again it was not so much as singed; which
very much aftonifhed 'em. One of them afked
her, what fhe thought of him; fhe answered,
" *the time will come, my Lord, when you fhall be
as low as I am, and that is low indeed* "This was
judged to be verified when *Thomas Lord Cromwell*, was beheaded. The Cardinal coming to
Cawood, afcended the Caftle-Tower, and taking
a prospect of the City of *York*, at eight miles
diftance, he vowed, when he came there he
would burn the *Witch*; but e'er he descended
the ftairs, a meffage arrived from the King to
demand his presence forthwith; so he was
obliged to return directly, and being took with a
violent loofnefs at *Leicester*, he gave up the
Ghoft in his Journey; which verified the prophecy.

Several others fhe delivered to different perfons
one of which was :—

Before * Ouze-Bridge *and* † Trinity-Church
*meet, what is built in the Day fhall fall in the
Night, till the higheft Stone of the* Church *be the
Loweft Stone of the* Bridge.

This came to pafs; for the Steeple was blown
down by a Tempeft, and the Bridge broke down

*A large Stone Bridge over the River *Ouze*, within the City of
York

† A Church fituate several hundred yards from the Bridge.

by a Flood occafioned by the Storm, and how it came to pafs we can't learn, that what they built in the Day fell down in the Night; but 'tis generally afferted it was fo; and it is certain that the top-Stone of the former Steeple is the foundation Stone of that part of the Bridge then rebuilt.

The fecond of this kind runs thus; *Time fhall happen, a Ship fhall fail upon the River Thames, till it reach the City of* London, *the Mafter fhall weep, and cry out, Ah! what a flourifhing City was this when I left it, unequalled through the World! but now fcarce a houfe is left to entertain us with a Flaggon.*

This was terribly verified when the City was burnt, *September* 1666, there being not *one* houfe left from the Tower to the Temple.

We now come to the Prophecies that occafioned this Publication, and which appear far to exceed *every thing* of the like nature extant.

A Copy of them was lately found amongft other Valuable Manufcripts the Property of a Gentleman deceafed, with this Title.

A Copy of a Collection of Prophecies delivered to the Abbot of Beverly, by Mother Urfula Shipton; the Original of which hath been preferved in Manufcript in a Noble Family thefe many Years

Years and was discovered among other curious and valuable Papers.

The Prophecies are as follow:—

About the Time that One *shall be,*
Join'd unto Two times Three,
And Four times Ten *with* Four times Two*,
Amongst us shall be great ado.
An Eagles Head *that time shall fall,*   5
And scatter sore his Young Ones *all.*
Then shall a Cypher *swell full great*
His Name †A Hundred *takes the Seat,*
And shall do mighty Things before,
He is removed off the Shore;   10
But Ten times Five *with* Two *and* Six,‡
Him in another World shall fix.
And quickly after you shall spy,
The Eagle *back again to fly.* §   15
He shall bedeck himself again,
With Feathers *on his* Father's Train.
'Till heavy Times shall make Men say,
Full oft' Alack! and Well-a-day.
And after all a Cloud *shall come,*
And almost darken quite the Sun,   20
And in that Time Actions shall be,
Chiefly driven on by Three,

* A. D 1648
† The Usurper Oliver Cromwell
‡ A. D 1658
§ Restoration of king Charles the second.

The

The Cross, *the* Surplice, *and the* Crown,
Strive who shall put each other down,
Great Treach'ry and Bloodshed then,   .   25
Shall sweep away great Store of Men,
The Lion *and blue* Flow'rs *shall Seek*
Quite to destroy th' Heretick Sheep,
And when the Cow *shall ride the* Bull,
Then Motly *Priest beware thy Skull.*   30
For a sweet Pious Prince *make room,*
And for the Kirk *prepare a* Broom.
Alecto next shall seize the Crown,
And Streams *of Blood run* Smithfield *down.*
A Maiden-Queen *full many a Year,*   35
Shall England's *warlike Scepter bear.*
The Western Monarch's *wooden* Horses,
Shall be destroyed by a Drake's Forces.
The Northern Lion *over* Tweed,
The Maiden-Queen *shall next succeed.*   40
And join in One *Two* Mighty States,
And then shall Janus *shut his* Gates.
Now England *soon is hard bested,*
Before the Mitre's *head be rid.*
False Ireland *contrives our woe,*   45
But zealous Scotland *doth not so.*
Rough Mars *shall rage as he were wood,*
And earth shall dark'ned be with blood.
Then will be sacrificed, C.
And not a king in England *be.*   50
But

But death shall snatch the Wolf *away,*
Confusion shall give up its sway,
And fate to England *shall restore,*
A king to reign as heretofore.
Triumphant death rides London *thro';*   55
And men on tops of houses go.
J. R. *shall into saddle slide,*
And furiously to Rome *shall ride.*
The Pope *shall have a fatal fall,*
And never more distress Whitehall.   60
A queen shall knit both North *and* South,
And take away the 'Luce's *tooth.*
A Lion-Duce *shall after reign,*
And of the Whiskers *clear the main.*
But he that chanceth to survive,   65
Shall see Old England *mainly thrive.*
England's *wonder which ne'er hath been,*
Three queens *in* England *shall be seen.*
Two dukes *shall for the crown contend,*
And bring the M————y *to end.*
B————s *shall fall into contempt and scorn,*
And Gospel Anglers *shall the* Kirk *adorn.*
If any ask, how these things come to pass;
The Fox *shall ride the* Goose, *the* Goose *the* Ass.

URSULA SHIPTON.

The greateft part of what has been hitherto publifhed under the title of *Mother Shipton's* prophecies, plainly appears to be no more than imperfect bits and fcraps of this collection, carried away, perhaps, in the memory of fuch as might, fometime have the opportunity of feeing it in the Noble Family where it was depofited The whole feems entirely to point at the *great events* that already have, and yet may happen to both church and ftate in this, and the neighbouring nations.

───────────────

EXPLANATION of the DIFFERENT PROPHECIES.

The firft thirty verfes feem to relate to the difafters that fhould befal great part of *Europe*, during the time of King *Henry* VIII. For the 29th and 30th verfes terminate in his reign, and are the laft wherein *that* reign can be underftood to be hinted at.

Verfe 29. *And when the* cow *shall ride the* bull

This feems to have been fulfilled when *Henry* VIII. married Lady *Anna Bullen;* for he, as Duke of *Richmond*, placed the *cow* in his arms, and the creft of her family was a black *bull's* head.

V. 30. *Then*

V. 30. *Then motly* priest *beware thy skull.*

Presently after the king's marriage, the seizure of Abbey Lands, &c. and the dissolution of monasteries ensued; whereby the *skull*, or *head-pece* of the priesthood (i. e. *gain)* was miserably broke.

V. 31. *For a sweet* pious prince *make room.*

By this, doubtless, is meant King *Edward* VI. a part of whose character is thus given by the learned Dean *Echard*, in his History of *England:* " He was truly just and merciful in his disposi- " tion; and took special care of the petitions " that were given him by the poor and oppressed. " But his zeal for religion crowned all the rest ; " which did not proceed from an angry *heat*, " but from a *real tenderness* of conscience, " founded on the love of God, and his fellow " creatures."

V. 32. *And for the* *Kirk *prepare a* broom.

This alludes to the beginning of the refor- mation; when many superstitions were *swept* out of the church.

V. 33. Alecto *next shall seize the crown.*

Alecto was one of the fabulous *furies* of the Heathen; whose employment was to kindle war, and distress mankind. She is here placed for Queen *Mary* I. In whose reign, as it is alluded

* A *North* country word for *Church.*

to

to in the 34th verse, the blood of the Glorious
Protestant Martyrs was plentifully shed in
Smithfield.

V. 35 and 36.

A maiden queen, *full many a year,*
Shall England's *warlike scepter bear.*

By these are meant Queen *Elizabeth,* who
reigned 44 years, 4 months and 6 days, upon
whom *Andrew Marvel* has left the following
verses :—

" *The other day fam'd* Spencer, *I did bring,*
" *In lofty notes* Tudor's *bless'd race to sing;*
" *How* Spain's *proud powr's her* Virgin-Arms
        " *controull'd,*
" *And golden days in peaceful order roll'd;*
" *How like ripe fruit, she dropp'd from off her*
        " *throne,*
" *Full of grey hairs, good deeds, and great re-*
        " *nown* "

Verses 37 and 38.

The Western Monarch's wooden Horses,
Shall be destroyed by a Drake's *Forces.*

The *Western Monarch* is supposed to mean the
King of Spain, whose Country lies on the West
side of the Continent, and his *wooden Horses*
his Fleet of Ships, or *Armada,* vanquished by
the *Brave* Admiral *Drake* and the rest of the
Queen's Forces, in the Year 1588.

Verses

Verses 39 and 40.

The Northern Lion, *over Tweed,*
The Maiden Queen *shall next succeed.*

The *Northern Lion;* i. e. King James I. born in *Scotland,* called a *Lion* not in consideration of any great Heroisms he should perform, but because the *Lion* is the principal Figure in the *British* Arms; whence the *King,* as the principal Person in the Realm, metaphorically takes the Name.

Verses 41 and 42.

And Join in One Two mighty States,
Then shall Janus *shut his Gates.*

The first bears an Allusion to the Uniting of the Two Crowns of *England* and *Scotland* in One, in the Person of King James. And the second, points out the *Peaceful Reign* of that Monarch, by shutting the Gates of *Janus;* who was one of the Heathen Gods, and the Gates of whose Temple were never shut but in time of Peace.

Verses 43 and 44 seem to hint at some great Calamities that should befall this Nation before the Deposition of Episcopacy, in the Reign of the *Republican Anarchy,* under the *Usurper* Oliver *Cromwell.*

Verses

Verses 45 and 46.

False Ireland *contrives our Woe,*
But zealous Scotland doth not so.

Doubtless these intended the *execrable* Massacre
in *Ireland*, in the Reign of King *Charles* I.
And the Loyalty of the *Scotch* in not joining the
Irish Rebels, but suffering with the *English*.

Verses 47 48 49 and 50.

Rough Mars *shall rage as he were *wood,*
And Earth shall dark'ned be with Blood.
Then will be sacrificed, C,
And not a King in England *be.*

This was verified in the time of the Grand
Rebellion, and *most unnatural* Civil War, when
the Nation was torn and pillag'd, the Laws
broke, the Constitution overturned, the King
and Monarchy *most execrably* Slain together.

Verses 51 52 53 and 54.

But Death shall snatch the Wolf *away;*
Confusion *shall give up the Sway;*
And Fate to England *shall restore,*
A King *to Reign as heretofore.*

If we can guess right, the first of these Verses
alludes to the Death of the usurper Oliver
Cromwell, who is very properly depicted as a
Wolf; and the other three to the Restoration
of King Charles the second.

* Mad.

Verses

Verſes 55 and 56.

Triumphant Death rides London thro'
And Men on Tops of Houſes go.

The firſt in all appearance, points out the terrible Plague that raged in *London* A. D. 1665 The ſecond circumſtantially alludes to the dreadful Fire in the Year following; ſignifying that People ſhould be obliged to run from one Houſe to another, over the Tops of the Houſes, to ſave themſelves, and their Effects.

Verſe 57 J. R. *ſhall into Saddle Slide.*
J. R. i. e. *James Rex.* or *King James* 2nd who aſcended the Throne upon the death of King Charles II.

V. 58. *And furiouſly to Rome ſhall ride*
Scarce was he ſettled upon the Throne, before he went to Maſs publickly; and, by purſuing imprudent and illegal Meaſures, was the Cauſe of the Verification of

Verſes 59 60.

The Pope *ſhall have a fatal fall,*
And never more distreſs Whitehall.

For he was abdicated for his Mis-goverment, and his Son-in-Law King *William* and Queen *Mary* II. were placed upon his Throne.

V. 61. A Queen *ſhall knit both North and South.*

This

This feems to refer to the Union of *England* and *Scotland* in the Reign of Queen *Ann*.

V. 62, *And take away the* 'Luce's *Tooth*.

This likewife feems to relate to her extraordinary Victories over *Lewis* 14th King of *France*; who we judge to be intended here by the *Luce*, which by way of Allufion, might here be put for *Flower de Luce*, the Arms of that Monarchy

Verfes 63 64.

A Lion-Duce *fhall after Reign*,
And of the Whifkers *clear the Main*.

What is meant by the *Lion Duce* may be matter of amusement to the curious, but as the word *Duce* sometimes reprefents the number *two,* so *two* in this ambiguous phrase may intend the fimilar word *second*, and our present Gracious Sovereign,* being the *second Lion* (or Englifh Monarch) of his name, it is far from being unlike'y that he may be the Prince here pointed out who shall clear the main of the *Whifkers*, which is a Northern term for *Mustachioes*, and doubtlefs alludes to the *Spanifh*, whose fafhion it has been for many centuries paft to wear them. But as this appears to relate to the

* The explanation of the above verfe was taken from an edition of Mother Shipton's Prophecies, printed in the reign of King George the Second.

prefent

present age, we leave it to the fkilful and ingeni-
ous, as we likewise do the following lines,
which feem to predict something further below
than the reach of the present age.

Whether the prophecy of the *Lilly* be *Mother
Shipton's* or no, we can't certainly determine,
but as it has been attributed to her, and is writ
in a peculiar sublimity of sense and ftile, we
think it would be very improper to omit it. It
runs as follows.

A CURIOUS PROPHECY

The Lilly *fhall remain in a merry World; and
he fhall be moved againft the seed of the* Lion ;
*and he fhall ftand on one fide of his Country with
a number of fhips. Then shall come the* son of man,
having a fierce Beaft *in his arms; whose King-
dom is the Land of the* Moon, *which is dreaded
throughout the whole World. With a number of
people fhall he pafs many Waters and fhall come to
the Land of the* Lion, *looking for help of the* Beaft *of
his Country. And an* Eagle *fhall come out of the
Eaft, spread with the Beams of the* Son of Man
and fhall deftroy Caftles of the Thames; *and
there fhall be Battles among many Kingdoms.
That year fhall be the Bloody field, and* Lilly,
F. K. *fhall lose his Crown; and therewith fhall*
be

be Crowned the Son of Man K. W. *and the fourth year shall be many Battles for the faith, and the* Son of Man, *with the* Eagle *shall be preferred, and there shall be an universal Peace over the whole World;* and there *shall be plenty of fruits; and then shall he go to the* Land of the Crofs.

———————

Whether the accomplishment of the above Prophecy be past, or to 'come we cannot ascertain. It appears to be very deep and Mysterious; we therefore leave it to Persons of profounder Penetration and superior Judgment.

We are informed, the last Prediction of our famous Prophetefs, was concerning the time of her own death; which 'tis said she declared to several who visited her in her advanced Age; and when the time she Prophecied of, approached, she called her friends together, advised them well, and took a Solemn leave of them, and, laying herself down on her Bed, she departed with much Serenity, A. D. 1651 being upwards of seventy Years of Age, after her death a Monument of Stone was erected to her Memory; in the high North-Road betwixt the Villages of *Clifton* and *Skipton,* about a mile

distant

diſtant from the City of *York*, (see the plate)
The Monument represents a Woman upon her
knees, with her hands closed before her, in a
praying poſture, and ſtands there to be seen to
this day. The following is said to have been her

Epitaph,

Here lyes ſhe who never ly'd,
Whoſe skill often has been try'd,
Her Prophecies ſhall ſtill ſurvive,
And ever keep her name alive.

So here we muſt take leave of the Courteous
Reader,

FINIS.

[Entered at Stationer's Hall.]